My Family

by Mario García

NATIONAL GEOGRAPHIC

Hampton-Brown

National Geographic and the Yellow Border are registered trademarks of the National Geographic Society.

WCN: 01-100-414

National Geographic School Publishing
Hampton-Brown
www.NGSP.com

ISBN: 978-0-7362-7985-7

Print Number: 6   Print Year: 2024
Printed in Mexico

Acknowledgments and credits continue on the inside back cover.

Who is this? This is my mother.

father

Who is this? This is my father.

sister

Who is this? This is my sister.

Who is this? This is my brother.

grandma

Who is this? This is my grandma.

grandpa

Who is this? This is my grandpa.

This is my family!